A VIOLENCE

PRINCETON SERIES OF CONTEMPORARY POETS

Rowan Ricardo Phillips, *series editor*

For other titles in the Princeton Series of Contemporary Poets,
see the end of this volume.

Also by Paula Bohince

Swallows and Waves
The Children
Incident at the Edge of Bayonet Woods

A VIOLENCE

POEMS

Paula Bohince

Princeton University Press
Princeton & Oxford

Copyright © 2025 by Paula Bohince

Princeton University Press is committed to the protection of copyright and the intellectual property our authors entrust to us. Copyright promotes the progress and integrity of knowledge created by humans. By engaging with an authorized copy of this work, you are supporting creators and the global exchange of ideas. As this work is protected by copyright, any reproduction or distribution of it in any form for any purpose requires permission; permission requests should be sent to permissions@press.princeton.edu. Ingestion of any IP for any AI purposes is strictly prohibited.

Published by Princeton University Press
41 William Street, Princeton, New Jersey 08540
99 Banbury Road, Oxford OX2 6JX

press.princeton.edu

GPSR Authorized Representative: Easy Access System Europe - Mustamäe tee 50, 10621 Tallinn, Estonia, gpsr.requests@easproject.com

All Rights Reserved

ISBN 9780691277776

ISBN (pbk.) 9780691277769

ISBN (web PDF) 9780691277844

ISBN (e-book) 9780691287393

Library of Congress Control Number: 2025934782

British Library Cataloging-in-Publication Data is available

Editorial: Anne Savarese and Emma Wagh
Production Editorial: Theresa Liu
Text and Jacket / Cover Design: Haley Jin Mee Chung
Production: Lauren Reese
Publicity: Jodi Price and William Pagdatoon
Copyeditor: Jodi Beder

Cover image: © Photo Josse / Bridgeman Images

This book has been composed in Adobe Garamond Pro and Scala Sans OT

10 9 8 7 6 5 4 3 2 1

CONTENTS

Accordion Music 1

Cradle Language 3

Escape to Fiji 4

The Lambs Are Not for Sale 5

Among Barmaids 7

Study of Beet and Earring 9

Black Cat 10

The Arbor 11

I Love the Whole World 13

Afterglow 15

Pillow Talk 16

Januaries 18

Glass of Milk 19

Eelish 20

The Egg of Anything 21

Lamentation Once Again 22

Ouroboros 24

Fruitless 25

Everything 26

At Thirty 27

Testimony 29

Blue Morpho 30

Color Theory 31

Two Donkeys in Eternal Rain 32

Marrow's in Vogue 33

Black Swans 34

Sumptuary   35

Restoration   36

Epic Rain   38

Search Field   40

The Bee, 2050   41

A Brief History of the Cocktail   42

Explicit, 1976   43

Lackluster, 2002   44

Elk Moving, Midnight in the Great Sand Dunes   45

Red Lake   46

The News   47

The End   49

A Violence   51

Untitled, 1954   53

The Skunk   54

Songbird   57

Quiet   58

Another Language   60

The Letdown   61

Horizon   62

Arcade   63

The Bat   65

Albino Deer   67

Pathway   68

Bluebird   69

Pokeweed   70

Ecce Homo   72

The Green   73

Acknowledgments   75

FOR PATRICK

ACCORDION MUSIC

The homestead was the whole of their wealth,
and it was much mud, and it was
cement crack and stump, stink of tar and bee-stung
pump, and it was

handed down like a seed pouch
or lye-combed baby clothes or this
warmed-up hearse
through whose bellows I levitated

in its *Please* and jolly heave,
an anvil strapped to Baby King,
in his eighties, who lived the breadth of his life
there, runt of six living brothers

and one sister of granite, Aunt Urša who kept house
for a family and got to visit the cape once
a year to mind the children,
a silence who swept the glass when I

went flying and wore an apron of cabbage
roses and closed her eyes to the whine
of the porch glider and rested.
White hair and baldness, they were Queen

Anne's lace, sprung everywhere,
leaning in, unknowable. Sure, I was eternal.
I was barely on Earth.
If they had emotions or motives

or tonics for the limp
or black lung or heart condition,
I didn't know them. By tipsy polka, I floated
as the rhubarb's grit on my tin held steady

beside kielbasa and pierogi.
We were ignorant
as sunshine, illiterate
King strapped to his box and my doomed

daddy in clover, in blown beer foam
like dandelions in July. Motes
now, my people, but a melody guided us
as it once brightened the edge of a Slovenian lake

where a girl held her hem
and waded in, our lives
inside of her and inside of him, the one
who held out his hand, the husband.

CRADLE LANGUAGE

Frill of cloud, a *Her* in the blue endless. Uneven hammering,
tantrum, panting, axe overhead in weightless indecision. Grimness
rushing from a well, numb feet and hands *(gone),*
milky mouth sour, a ropewalking spider
touching dolly's raggedy head, skull plates fusing. First snow:
paint shook from sill with each blow. Tip-to-tail jolt of cuckoo.

ESCAPE TO FIJI

Swimming in a mirage, past the bull shark, sicklefin
lemon, buoyed by a personalized ocean, psychosis floating
me when I wearied, rescued thus by blue saturation,
perfumed and pumicing element, living
as on that Styx song in adolescence, trance overtaking fear
on the papasan chair,
the same biblical sentence cycling
until it engraved on my brain God's authority. I turned
the watery page. I went to the sun unashamed, submitting to new
species: boggling palms, animals like drawings.

Say *toxin* again. Under a dome of *aura,* swirl over me
noni soap. Oils of frangipani,
verbena, gifted by the last true friend, color me in.
Flowers, include me ecstatic in your orgasm.
Opening spheres of vistas, let me buckle with, at ease
as clownfish or mollusk. Erase me
lotioning little sister's behind-the-ears, years of weeping
scales, skin like vellum, her head on my lap, our systems changing
permanently, in stress. Benumbed, watching beauty queens
departing an airplane, sisterly in leis and sashes.

THE LAMBS ARE NOT FOR SALE

Despite the mildness of sea-glass eyes,
clear brows, their bodies entire, flocked with white-
tongued clover, in clover, panting after
mothers, arched under the creamy ceilings of
clouds-in-frescoes bellies,

the lambs are not for sale.
When sleepy, they curl into the porcelain figures
your grandmother kept on her dresser.
Entranced by placid poses, how long you looked
at her collection, at the separate world.

Long ago, you studied the milk-carton
children, their crooked haircuts
and freckles, the optimism of their last
school picture, that they were and were not you,
and now the lambs stir that feeling

of rescue, but they are not for sale. You survived,
those children froze as milk did
on winter's doorstep. Your mother
gave you the rich cork if you shared with
the baby, who now lives apart.

How strong the cues to reassemble
all of you in that house, each set like a doll

with a small wooden spoon. The lambs do this,
make you sidle up and remember.
You named one Precious and one Nostalgia,

but they're not for sale. The urge to ribbon
them with blues and pinks,
delicate as the ones threaded through Marie
Antoinette's underthings, collides with reminders
to read more, and in French,

but you're so weary in the evenings
all you can do is watch television. If it comforts,
she made a similar wonderland
in Petit Trianon, nursery of girlhood innocence,
and her children were still killed.

That's why the lambs aren't for sale.
Hold fast to the fantasy: their inviolate curls
the foam of seashore summers, wished-on fluff of dying
dandelions, the eyelet of a christening gown
pulled over your infant eyes.

AMONG BARMAIDS

There was a metal door that took both hands
of a strong man to open,

but we did it daily. Inside were our charges, sealed in
submarine darkness. We swam

through their booze, past the pool
table's alien island, darts that *thwacked* the pricked wall

like failure itself, spinning like downed ducks
to the filthy tile. Like good dogs, we fetched them.

In a windowless silence, we watched our drunks
bend like sycamores in an all-day snowstorm.

When they slept, we let them, then shook them
with the tenderness of mothers.

They woke and smoked, still dreaming, wore their trade
on their fingers—coal or dirt or grease.

On the jukebox, five songs repeated, each a lament
about cheating women. We hummed along,

bore the plodding joke, slurred compliment,
nodded at creased photographs of estranged children.

The beer rose in gushes. Our forearms bulged.
One girl, what she wanted before she died

was to see the ocean. Froth pillowed up
from underground barrels, by pipes and pulleys.

We wore out our pity, watching men stroke the bar
like the hardened brushed hair of a daughter.

We wore ours in scarves. Our hoop earrings swayed
on the downbeat. We held rags

or tucked them in jeans, tattooed the names
of ex-husbands, first lovers, into our skin

in script so thick and Bible-elaborate as to be illegible.
One wore her drugged-out son's childhood face

on her wrist, his doomed grin following us.
Men brought their kids when the wives needed peace.

We gave them Cokes and bowls of cherries,
let them draw on napkins and pinned up the drawings.

Sometimes, we spun them on the make-believe dance
floor, trying to turn despair into a party.

STUDY OF BEET AND EARRING

Vegetable fuchsia but faded, gilt
gone bad from its season in Hell. Plucked up
with dirt on its cheek, petrified
as a rose shut in a box and dull as a brain
left too long in one place.
Sedate glamour on the counter, the brass in me
unhinged from my skin: golden
chime, little tower. Truth is, I've been
walking, figuring the ladder of how each year
held together. The boy I slept with
in a single bed, a single embrace, was one:
sexless, lust-filled, lonely as the taproot
on the table, weird as the earring
found in a thrift store, gold plate already flaking,
atoms of it anointing the straw chair
and spider plant, its babies beginning to crawl.
I went crazy, sought out the lunatics,
drove to the bar and pried open the door,
the men inside gesturing *Come in,*
wanting a woman. Passed the pit bull
tied to the porch of my neighbor who's faking
paralysis for insurance, photographers creeping
in the weeds to catch him walking.
His gram smoked her pipe and swung
on a swing where his dog now barks
ruthlessly. She grew me beets and other gifts,
then the world ordered *Weep,* and I wept.

BLACK CAT

Hit, besieged by miniscule
and spirited soldiers pillaging blood
for heat and nutrients,
the pillow of it rising, volatile
in sun, then sinking moodily into tar and the tar
it's becoming, though its four identical
brothers and sisters still stalk the corn
as always, or perch spookily in the neighbor's tree, or sleep
in the salvage, beneath a trailer
shuttered against the ongoing progression
of animus to compost
to cosmos, though the human
must feel it, driving over what was once his
toward the junkyard's offer
of day labor: pulling rust from rust,
delivering unto his own mailbox
the township's advisories and legal arguments
on traces of lethal compounds
while the animal's engrossed in its own
slow going. No dreamy eye to recognize, no ear
to hear its kin fight awfully, same as ever, over the cars'
midnight whispers of *passion, passion.*
Impossible to imagine less. Impossible
to rest with the agony of its siblings caught
in a death grip, bawling like babies.

THE ARBOR

In August, didn't I twist
inside the crib of its shade, maternal curls
and woody veins, *gone away*
beneath filigree grave-
big, to compete with crow
and beetle—nameless, at ease
in the callous nothing from which the grapes
emerged and multiplied?
I suckled dusty otherness,
nuzzled against skins and found
each body a font.
Souls hardened in them, filthy
and untended. They lived, they shivered
in sun as I did, at the whim
of feral people
agog at mewling daughters.
How we swam in the humid
flex and murk.
We swooned and shook.
Our hearts, O our hearts beneath the Xs
that held up vines like a fainting child
were anguished, the quiet after
anguish, also. Quaking
fists, the warning, rising scream,
telephone ringing.
Kin to the stunned doe, she

folded into limbs. He
was the snake's retreat, brooding
in loamy rooms. Hypnotized
by heat that could not
break, we succumbed. Jug and jelly
wasted, un-tongued,
on the table. No voices shaping love words,
no song the dappled doorway
of arbor restored.

I LOVE THE WHOLE WORLD

After Agnes Martin

Gasp in the mothering quiet. In light, in softness,
a spider breathed at my breast.

Who will mother me? When?

How it lounged on the cream of my blouse.
I undid my barrette then.

Empathetic, abstract, near, how inside the colors went.

How I wept.

When prettiness left, there was only voice,
vaporous above ocean at daybreak.

Beach sleep, cloud sling, cashmere feeling.

Blush, sand, apricot, lemon,
but lighter, rinsed of those associations.

I sat on a bench, in a daze. In that place, it was ocean
all around. Shipwrecked, bone-buttoned, bedded.

Where the pretties released, pearl and peach,
blue-white, salt-rinsed. I was softly awake, soft as *love*

leaving a mouth. And meant.

AFTERGLOW

Ache of un-stabled horses at sundown, winter-
berry turned up to ten. Escaping the tent's nylon into
the frost's first breath, I thought,
It's the wanderings between stars, those leaps
that mean everything. Marzipan
skin of Melissa in her red gingham bikini, afloat in the black
zero. Me: febrile, sunburnt, eyes
like wheels in the motel mirror. Our hair
whipping the currents alongside her white 'vette, salt-
pricked, Mariah's whistle notes levitating us
above hot tar. Shirtless carpenters on their summer jobs,
on scaffolding, flexing *(slowness),* oiled as horses.

PILLOW TALK

Snowflakes become cutlasses, the *thousand cuts* death.
Dose of Valium, again: double negative, beveled ambiance.
Harlequin-faced deer, say *cerulean*
before ambushing the field, startling the horses
carousing in jackets. Sensations,
shimmy through an hourglass. Transform night's abstract ice
into the surrealist's melt. Quiet the motor
of the getaway car. Hack the forest
to reach the morels' kaleidoscope. Nibble moss on all fours.
This is a thought. Think that in distress. Dupe the dreadful
otherwise. Be not the breakable fawn,
motherless and quaking. Remember the balm
of penmanship lessons, content above a sea of cursives.
Sleep inside the inky light-
house of *I.* Imagine the throat-high grasses
of vetiver, oil skimmed from water,
bottled to calm the boat-body. Ride off
on the promised pony, your essence on the reins.
Lay down the knuckled keys. No harm came
then, though you were dreamy, disturbed, ill-prepared, scared
at all the wrong moments: parties, Christmas mornings.
Quaint, quaint goes the weather against the window.
Succumb to its undertow as the soprano
pipistrelles awake from hibernation to gorge on moths, filling

the dark with their decibels. Remember Ebba,
her apple tart with cream made for your hospital homecoming,
humming moon of her face, who painted your bedroom
doorknob the merciless sun of her childhood village.

JANUARIES

A cold most lethal, the pine
if looked at long enough. My ice vision,
crown of deer inside, beheld, coats smoldering,
and one valiant cardinal above
stringing invisibles. When it becomes
unbearable, I'll describe this in the colors of
a children's book. Winters with Annie
playing orphans in the woods: foraging, peeling
hours in all those blades beneath a bitter
lemon sun, made sweet by not being alone.
Enter, snow. One dissociation sifts over
another, with decades between, hooves retreating
into the past, whatever that is, the cold
accumulating all its meanings.

GLASS OF MILK

Was a swell commandment: drink up, sleep. She'd
relinquished the vampy black and absconded to her toddler
color *(muddy sunset)* as we, one from each grief stage,
commissioned to flock her, petal'd her pale strapless,
pressed the appliqué along her spine with dancer's glue,
all funds sunk into that silk, hence the wan hors d'oeuvres,
sheepish flasks, *White Album* on a loop.
Eventual brood snug in her ova, she straightened, candle-
brave before that noonday deadline. Startled nipples
got plastered. A dose of almonds
so no swooning during *forevers*. Preview
of losing it, Skyping with her guru
to parse the voice of God, thunderstruck into the nib of
a midcentury housewife. Waking rapturous, un-entombed,
to commune with birdsong and him in the mystical
five am. An Oona holding hydrangeas, she was. Soon
to vanish into a strobing, off-kilter rainstorm,
the frothy whitecaps of a harbor's embrace and resistance.
There stands her hometown man. A future of borax-
bleached nappies, the Paxil. She turned us a keen look
sailing down satin. Absolute abandonment, *can't come with,*
the fox's grin plunging unabashed into snowdrift.

EELISH

Stricken, seen, satellite at the edge of a party,
being fifteen, with the black bulbs someone's planted
in the mother's lamps to give glow-in-the-dark
ambiance to hideous kisses, and the ruffles
are all wrong on the saved-for shirt, and the curtains,
suave in the murk, seem to laugh. The liquidy
fin of feeling is destination-less, twisting
like paper wrapped 'round a pinkie
in blind date anticipation. Toy for
the psyche, phrase to swim through the mind
like an offense, at three am.
Half-helix, as if waiting for, *Oh God, don't
say it,* a soul mate. What sheathes the stealth
bomber has something of its skin. Pastiche of pluck
and terror, nerve faltering halfway. Opposite
of starlight, stagnant brook that drowned Ophelia, jpeg
from a former colleague on holiday, landed in spam,
looking older and captioned, *Well, here I am.*

THE EGG OF ANYTHING

is holy, molten in its calcium
cup, sun and moon mixed, hot
in its prison, cells'
incentive to fuse firing, no
second to loiter, calling
now to a predator's jaw. How
the genetic vow is kept.
Jellied not-yet,
hard as thought becoming
belief, little o
in *hope* or *love*, un-
umbilical one, cast into air,
mother gone, father
long gone, *uh-huh* goes your
heart, that dummy *yes* said from
a soul agog at such splendor.

LAMENTATION ONCE AGAIN

Though I began as shudder through the father,
uncurling terror, growing toward light, finally sleepwalking
as shock-riddled bafflement, leaning against
a vacancy. Though I was silence and rise
and deliverance through icy rinse to arrive and be stood still as the dead
in the blizzard's deeps, Frostian echoes
and presence of wedding bullets sent up in spring
fallen back as wintry confetti,

birch-fog and memory: a hand eternal *(patient, veined)*
guiding me toward the awful,

and then the moment's over.

I came with a gun, my bleak inheritance, to shoot
above juncos unbridled from pines. *I just can't leave
his bones behind.* What I said
to the years-gone-by beloved. And didn't,
circling decades around them,

embracing disintegration: greenish
stubble, collapsed wool suit, helpless mind long leaked out of ears,
all he was dust or mist. Jesus,

I was afraid as a jay against glass, ashamed to have
a body at all. It is the doe

(always, always) I come back to. Her guileless,
maternal face, her breast a candle
against the shroud and christening dress
of vapor. Absurdly alive we were,
ceding the field, its hymnal-thin pages, to a hypnotic gentleness.
Thoroughly in the world,

curious of the world,

the *why* dooming us gently, hope and pain in every utterance of that
hurt, over and over unanswered, flowering
like snowdrops underneath the snow.

OUROBOROS

Frigid in vibrating daylight, with no distinction
between indoors and out, Ailene on the gurney
asked her children, *Am I dying?* and received
a coward's answer. How she eyed the ward, panicked,
more alive than ever. Once a lounging

teenager, biting the brush end of her braid,
the lattice more alive than ever with carnations.
Braised rabbit hunted that morning, not sleeping, no
indeed, beneath silver. Relieved of instinct.
Retold in a tempo to correct the grievous echo.

FRUITLESS

A grief of salt over a deer's last leap, collapse of
that crystal palace over the fatal synaptic blink, risen
into a fifth day of indignity. Absolved,
she softens. The township's embossed her
with acid. Unhinged, she is: pelt split, within visible, sting
dissolving acts: nosing apples, lying with sisters.
Fractals disguise the isolate body.
Why me? is a fruitless question, and dangerous.
Snowflakes touch her unseeing eye, the feminine tense,
It had been before it never was and never will be again.

EVERYTHING

When the shiver's erased from winter, sci-fi algae
seize on weakness, pop-and-locking unstoppable cover
over the hemlock's shading branches,
smothering in situ sap, leaf, the once robust
becoming skeletal, and what remains offers its frailty
over the withering river, wavelet
a wavering domino
as trout in full sun gasp, gills twitching
in heat, dim oxygen to feed
their flourish and flimsy. Spring trembles
like a bomb packed with snowmelt, its all-at-once
shaking trout eggs from mud, spun
like rice on the floor, that human error. The famous
butterfly poised on a twig, she lifts and leaves, dressed
in gold and jet—chic—changing everything.

AT THIRTY

At thirty, I fled from my life
in a hailstorm and firestorm, into what
I termed *the big rest,*

unpacked at my mother's house,
slept in my sister's bed,
signed up to swim at the Y, swam twice

daily, in the mornings
with patients doing recovery exercises
in the shallow end,

afternoons hung the damp suit,
black flag, on the line,
microwaved a meal, then napped,

the sleep my calamine, chlorine
my medicine, my weakness everywhere,
I could barely stand,

I swam the evenings, before closing,
reciting poems silently
from the mind's anthology,

I was alone, backstroking
through that humid chamber, beneath
frescoes of dolphins and nymphs,

I floated, a baby in her crib,
mesmerized by those gentle images—
for a long time it was like this.

TESTIMONY

The cardinal and jay appeared at the crisis—

totems speaking in low human voices, daggers dressed in winter's
rich coats, snow-trimmed, looking coldly at me.

To be a child in the eye of a blizzard, there is no center.

My friends were the only clear things—
classic and gemlike, immune to self-hatred or the wormy sickness
accomplishment brings.

One angel, one demon,
they each took a shoulder, arguing my worth.

I sat down in the ice and divested myself of questions. Did I fear
for my life in those earliest years? *Every day,*
a voice answered, *in every aspect.*

BLUE MORPHO

Adrift in an azure trance, affixed by invisible
star-points of pins to the sumptuous nothing of black
velvet, it's as immense as the word *once*
uttered once, buffeted by silence, to float or sink.
Gazing into the pool-like body, how slowly it becomes
the coffined loved one—exotic, exhausted, ex-
everything. Small as Earth on television, then realer:
the otherworldly waters of Iceland flown over
once, the shifting blues frightening in their nearness,
the glorious black shore. You, afraid until the sensation
of a longed-for presence hit, better than morphine.
You clapped with the rest—reborn, exhilarated.

COLOR THEORY

And I'm alone in Cornwall, squinting
with a 99, the sky doing that dizzying thing again,

someone's mother in a maroon maillot
cooing to a starfish, giving glimpse to

the therapist gone to Jawbone in her Honda,
following a voice. Sara

in her apartment held the lilac, lavender,
indigo to my neck. *You're a Summer,*

she'd said. How safe I felt then,
The Conversation on VHS, beneath immense

paintings, all celery shades, expressing
post-divorce clarity, fields and auras,

one kitten in the tin ceiling tiptoeing
rain, the other adamant for kisses. The loveseat,

the tea, the Tarot unfinished, the talking
that felt limitless, you know? Locked in *(gold*

slid), no longer anonymous, from a bosom
of incense and secrecy, I grew.

TWO DONKEYS IN ETERNAL RAIN

Lopsided in the crag, in the sticky realm of pagan
beehives, their honorable heads precede bodies that seem sewn
of soaked felt, whitewash of teeth like the flat
tink, tink of highest piano keys in a barren house, in druidic
elderflowers. Their existence seems a rebuke of symmetry,
which is beauty boiled down. *If you're beautiful, you don't
wonder. People tell you.* And the frayed sun
shone and staggered in the up. In blue and red patchwork
blankets, they were a reincarnation of true wanderers under
the North Star. Whorl in the wood of the world. Little and Skellig
Michael risen in the opacity like the spines of monsters.

MARROW'S IN VOGUE

So the veal, watched over like a prodigy, gifts its last
possession. Stuff like February slush in hollows

must be coaxed by an oven to soften but not run away. We like it
better than butter, with parsley to cut the unctuousness.

We like to trim the byssus from the mussel, see trotters' toes
almost human in the cold with other bundled offal,

for fish heads to show us xylophones
below in dismal buckets. We stroke shocked eyes,

palm kidneys slippery as trumpets abandoned
in field grass by a defeated army, reborn into ragtime.

Paired with deep red, spread hot on toast, is a taste of privacy,
a ledger of losses, *Beyond* and *Before,* trembling incarnate.

BLACK SWANS

The next morning we met at the Lough, Aisling
and me, without the men. How relaxing.
Drenched as in pitch or ashes, the silhouettes floated by,
bred in Australia, nevertheless Irish. The mutes
might bully them, coral-billed as Audrey's signature
Breakfast at Tiffany's shade. We strolled behind the huge
wobbly wheels of the carriage. More fragile, stranger
than the cloudlike others. An emerald dream of money
had lingered, so it felt good to be awake
in the rain, her speaking Gaelic to the baby, waves
of babble soothing my limbic system.
Last night, at dinner, a male professor explained his
productivity as her nipples expressed milky flowers.
White marble of municipal buildings, statuesque obsidian
swan reflections sunk in the basin. What nouvelle
cuisine had arrived clattering from a gaggle of waiters?
Some frazzled egg adrift in the beet's magenta?

SUMPTUARY

Ravenous rain finishing through medieval
walls, crows and seagulls taking up then their mutual
pleasure positions. A flutter of nuns,
wimples uplifted when the gate finally opened.
Lent flat, one key, in a maze, on an island.

Cleopatra's suprasternal notch, that pearl-
dusted dimple, mother to the old French *gorgeous.*
The greyhound's coiled shyness, retreat. The maid's
gold eyetooth slowly seen. Double cream of
childhood amnesia, flushed beneath velveteen.

RESTORATION

A red-haired woman
bends over tapestry that is
also red, mostly
red, her face tense, downcast, what man
has torn asunder she
corrects, convex glass
between her breasts, pendulous
on its string.

Unless the thing
is medieval, historical, I
cannot see the need. But people,
some people, want it,
will pay handsomely.
Heirloom rugs and pillows.

At the end, my father
day-labored.
In a cold wind: him,
throwing boards with nails in them.
Gloveless, he does this.

The image rushes through
such wreckage
a brain becomes. Funeral flowers

cut down mid-bloom are flown, jarred
in the perfumed
room where his body rests,
at last, on satin.

EPIC RAIN

Ten hours of continuousness, the audio
promises, looped by a stranger
who's enhanced the thunder, embedded trickles
from pine needles as from syringes,

assembled clouds, vast and digital,
to perform his soundtrack, so that a million amygdalae
can relax together, the frazzled city centers
resetting to *Homo sapiens* smoothness,

and the far-flung, isolated bedrooms
begin filling with rain in the REM stage, and the delta
waves resemble the ones at sea,
after catastrophe,

a civilization's treasures floating
unencumbered: an Apollonian vase's athlete
submerged, the landscapes
and self-portraits jostling like rafts over falls,

the chiaroscuro and sfumato, impasto
passages tumbling through foam. This is the brain
on benzos and earphones, frictionless
and plugged in, miraculously,

to the seafloor's fiber optics, those tubes sometimes
touched in the gloomy gelatin by
a sucker, then withdrawn, of one who cradles
itself to sleep in all of its arms.

SEARCH FIELD

In underpants and undershirt, pink lambs printed on the weave, with me
stirring oatmeal at the sink is what I dream. What it means, the site reads, is
symbiosis: intimacy that never leads to sex. I'm safest in quiet one-way
meetings, sitting like a spider at the center of a web, watching it tremble.
    To rest
in the rocker and have the world widen to dream is to be blurred
as a baby watching her mother *clink* in the kitchen, background whispers of
belonging soothing a system. Unreal, it seems now,
the flock of sheep in the train window, first glimpse of Pennsylvania after
    breaking down
in New York. Five field-seconds perfected by fog, duffle snuggled against me
like a child, the wash of creamy daubs against green,
then gone. I've not moved for hours. Each opened tab lowers the temp.
I've traveled on a rail of fiber optics to quell the panic. *Click, click,*
fields go faster, accumulation of wool in the past, no shutdown, no forward.

THE BEE, 2050

The bee buries its memories—
mythic, implanted—
in holographic flowers,

bells flickering, aquiver with pixels,
the red silence of roses
coming to

as the bee dives for pollen
(like love restored
by technology, it tastes of honey-

lite, nearly heaven)
antennae tunneling deeper, the bee
almost actual, alas

its program whistles it back
to the lab, ancestral
thrum—thick, unguent—

still vibrating in its system
while the garden sleeps in a cloud,
touchless as imagination,

which rushes in like the kiss
of a boy in spring, or autumnal
illness, to fill a vacuum.

A BRIEF HISTORY OF THE COCKTAIL

Yes of forsythia against the limitless ivy, a nude posed in a garden
against the silver maple pinwheeling its children into a gown around her

chime of the cliff-hanging falcon's talons against a rabbit,
wheezing soldier in a field, gunpowder tainting the cake in his pocket

jet fuel over the Pacific, waking to a hula in a zephyr,
the bride deplaning onto an island chain, bowing to leis of plumeria

the mallow of nurses' shoes, their news, the black sedan of
a telephone spreading it like a virus and, after, the scent of a cedar closet

white gloves of a mare, in heat, pawing clover, the sail of a Spitfire
cresting a hill in San Francisco, fin against sunset

rosin on the cello's catgut, a honeycombed queen calling home
her lovers, a Basquiat above the head of an ascetic, chaos over order

magenta in the thorns, shy to the shears, making the blue jays bluer,
someone on the bed's chenille edge composing an oratorio of medicines

the bartender in his icepick scars twisting zest over his creation, wheel
and butane of his Zippo kissing as the citrus, at last, expresses

EXPLICIT, 1976

Oculus giving up Andromeda,
pulse of variegated phlox,

fog-drenched, a virginal shepherd on lamb
watch, terrine of fowl and gilled

chanterelles, cold enmeshment
of mare and filly, ecocide

laws, unforgiving
blistered forests of a once-

divided country, impasse
o'er a holiday, Isle of Man

or the Canaries, *Ah*
from Freud's Viennese clinic, opening

seam of teenaged wallpaper,
ultra-ambient

tiger prawns, a third martini, Tiger Lily
jealous in first edition luster.

LACKLUSTER, 2002

Isolatress of the Zinc Bar beside some bore
droning buckshot shenanigans,

Sartre, studded cheek
and rubble asmolder, gray matter jukeboxing

smoke into two tracks dubbed
Courgette and *Orchid,* fragment of the *Hey*

there grin of that girl on the sidewalk
on skates in New Orleans,

hologram of
every Esmé ever, corsage

affixed to the X,
antennae of xenon bulbs oracling

24/7 their apex luminescence, drinking in
the aftermath gratis mimosas,

reward for spilling a Tetris of yesses, spring's
tongue, *Go on,* on the very equinox.

ELK MOVING, MIDNIGHT
IN THE GREAT SAND DUNES

Red fans from flashlights, easy on animal eye.

Dunes ruffle like pages uplifted one afternoon, the future
close and restless. The sand

remakes itself, AI-esque, and the wind-rush
of the herd comes before

it's visible, a presence
eternally moving, perceived by the snail

of cochlea, that harness,
which speaks to the ossicles and amplifies the miracle

until there's only blacker outlines against
the Milky Way's galactic pulse.

Crickets and kangaroo rats, gold-
eyed owls sequester in the crevices, with bobcats.

Elk drive past *(clatter and pant)*, a wallowing passing through
my passive, diurnal life: let in, joyful,

opposite of morbid.

RED LAKE

I feel as if I'm always on the verge of waking up.—Fernando Pessoa

Was spring, naturally, verve of fugitive colors finding voice,
and seeing subjects as they were: portrait of Pope Innocent X
in its own red room, the clasped couple in masks
(his edema hands, her nerves), and my shame, magma of
the first life coming fast to surface, and curious if Velázquez
used Red Lake or Madder or Opera for the cape. Enflamed, thinking of
the Negroni to be had on a terrace. In Florida, a red tide
stank the sand. Almost moved there before the virus. What a disaster
(Write it!) that would have been. Or is the road not taken
ruby-studded? Now I'm in the West, a mile closer
to the sun, its protons, plasma, and had the deepest dream last night
in the mountains. I was a cave dweller in a high-up cave
with two wolfy children. My mate (I thought like that) was huge,
asleep by the embers. The cave mouth held the lightest blue
of daybreak, a white glow. It rained a frail rain. I was at peace
inside the frame of my dream-painting, then woke and searched
for all the versions of Bacon's *Study after* . . .
Motionless travel. Like on that bench in Lisbon, the canary,
gold, mustard blur it was as I stuffed cherries in my mouth, tonguing
them as the red-naped woodpecker sucks its sap well and guards it
and makes the sound of a child crying, inconsolably red.

THE NEWS

An ultraviolet urchin *(planetary,*
local) was lulling unaware
in waves eternal

when Mari's email turned to
stardust, touching a satellite's face
for a nano, then

crystallizing on Earth
in the absolute blackness
of a laptop's clamshell,

in zone difference. The Pacific
tugged its trash as I
dreamt, as the crab

awoke shameless, shrugging
off its burial, beginning again.
The news unread

was a lizard clutching drift,
half-lidded, poised
in ancient sleep.

Red-eyed in the privacy
of a humming machine, a gasp
hovered. One luck-

less, rock-cracked brother,
out of time, was becoming else-
where on sand as cliff-

hanging gulls swung to
its gleam or glitch, ecstatic keen
of deadstick landings.

THE END

Beyond the furred plot
of reindeer moss
braced against ice-studded skid
is an opening
to the end:

valley of embodied
death illumed by glacial breath
and spines like ship-
wrecked missives.

But doesn't the king
eider keep company beside
the placid heart of musk ox?

Don't the fox and skua
conspire at the edge?

Leaf-ease between dwarf shrub
and Arctic willow
bit beneath crystals,

cormorants and terns
flanking melt

as a wolf spider descends a so-
called emptiness,
as something undiscovered rattles
bud and jut.

Instinct trembles
within the lichens' plurals,
arterial on rock, selves scribbling,
like us, each awe.

A VIOLENCE

As the spring peeper rushes
its performance,
as the chorus hoarsens before
a moony lens, as it pulses in the here
and elsewhere,

hiding in the dusty pond
of its skin, so the traumatized
child's amygdala reacts, gripped by
permanent panic,

grown weird in the woods
among broke iris, introvert
birches, the cones
of her eyes sorting *frond*
from *danger,* repainting the world,
the first memory:

Mother spun past the playpen,
hands like horse-blinders, panicked
by need, the baby's
shame smoldering for decades,

thus the toad becomes
maternal heartbeat, sanity in the *hence,*
when too much spring
is a violence,

melt overwhelming the brook,
crushing eggy nests, the fawn born
too soon, too weak

amid pinprick midges, sick
hemlock, and somewhere the helpless
one reaches still toward her savior,
urgent in the blurry *before*.

UNTITLED, 1954

After Mark Rothko

To land within a corona of jonquil, portal
to retrospect, with the immanence of insect. A thorax

hottens, sensational, in its own yellow canopy.
Being, flown via surprise winter *(at rest, in instinct)*

is diaphanous as a mother in the claw foot,
soot-charged, after axing a bureau. Calm comes in fog,

on greeny stem, inside the experiment. Blushes do
as sunrise does, solvent of having been seen.

Attached, swaying in ruffle. No wonder
humans prefer a certainty of square over circle

save a daiquiri's expansive rim, its lemony, boggling pith.
Occultish, any opening that is mouth, ear, canal

to the airless underneath. Snow covers what was once
most personal. Energetic, *was* dissipates.

THE SKUNK

A smolder, an echo of shame, weary wick of it.

In the smudgy *Local* section, a fire
living underground for a half a century will be put out.
An ember once tossed into a mine shaft
within a mile of my house, some midnight by a tired
anonymous, that person surely dead now, the consequence
roaming since, low-lit at times as a candle,
other years ghost-vigorous.

I wanted to go to it, to feel the emotion
of it, the same impulse in the therapist's office, quiet
I don't knows lodged there.

Mornings of fog, crystalline memories, sympathetic roads.

I thought of the Italian modernist, like a brother
the winter I again took up smoking
to stand in the pristine and be belled over. In one poem,
he cupped a firefly, spark of childhood,
for *his* mother, and ran home at breakneck speed
to keep it illuminated.

I felt that. Exhausting myself,
plugging every leaking aspect of myself

for her smile, to wake her there at the table. Flicker
at the corner of her resisting mouth, and I went wild,
memorizing her the way others did *Ozymandias.*

One Christmas, when I was grown, I wanted to cook for her
the meal of a lifetime. To say, *Mom, This is living. This is love.*
Feel it. Flakes of salt on closed lips of asparagus,
duck limp-necked on a secondhand platter.

She kept her head down and ate fast, with shame, and gave me
before leaving melted together wedding rings,
hers and my dad's. Amulet for I don't know what.
Pain-medallion. Coin for the underworld.

In the New Year, I flattened beneath
the dentist's lead apron and thought of her (I'm always
thinking of her), her pilled red sweater, how she looked around
at the candles, her face scorched from crying.

O hiss of an iron releasing its malice as I sat on a dirty floor,
as she held it to my ear, whispering, *Your father prefers*
the bars to us. He won't (hiss) come home
because he hates us.

What a paradise we could have lived.

Now, by the smoking hole, inflections come faster.
Visionary rain and séance rain, sincere shawl
of rain as the skunk's wrapped in the shawl of herself, her off-
spring in the den where tree roots are dead,
and it's pathetic to live so near.

Shovel-headed, digging into the past, I work, I collapse, I lie
on a vibrating mat meant to mimic
the maternal embrace. The TV reads me a lullaby of recipes
in a voice soft as rain ceasing.

I sleep while fire seethes through the maze.

Imagine the ideal mother, the therapist said. He shifted when
I spoke an octave higher, when I cried out for
the mother's animal body and made a grotesque motion with my face,
meaning I wanted to burrow against it.

Sometimes, I did. Sometimes,
I placed her hand on my hand.

If I could build an ideal mother, calm
in linen, in sedate
earrings, would I?

Once, she appeared as Meryl Streep, in the field
where my real mother burned off her rage, and I was made to
follow, less than a dog on a leash. In the therapist's
office, among the smashed stalks, breathlessness, sweat,
Meryl said to me, *This sucks.*

Tender skunk-mother, I love you, receding
in your backward shuffle.

The songbirds are gone, disavowing the hellhole soon to be filled
with spring water or some alkaline compound:
balm of man, cold compassion.

56

SONGBIRD

The songbird sipped from a man-
made lake and couldn't discern
its poison. The world
blinkered like snow at night, and still
she performed her cadenza.

Now she lies beneath a briar,
in citrine satin, diva fallen mid-
act, to gasps, her eye
no longer avid but a black, glassy sea
edging an abandoned mansion.

QUIET

> North America's birds are disappearing from the skies at a rate that's
> shocking even to ornithologists. Since the 1970s, the continent has lost
> 3 billion birds.—Elizabeth Pennisi, *Science,* 2019

How quiet the skies, I hardly noticed, flitting from screen
to screen, scouring illuminated fields, possessed
as the headless finch Billy left me as a gift.

Pitched into the garden,
ribs revealed by July's relentless smile, it grew gloomy as a harp
after the girl's outgrown her childhood
bedroom, immense gold wing in all that pink
too heavy to lift.

This death? I weeded around it, wreathed it, spoke to it
as Woolf lay cheek to earth beside hers, as Hiroshige's
ink became bullfinch, canary, egret, black-naped
oriole and Java sparrow

while an aspen traveled through silt and gravel to cast shadows
here, traced in a daze on butcher paper, hoof-like leaves
galloping quietly over.

Above my drawings, comic warblers,
spoonbills and thrushes, swifts asleep in the chimney's *tut tut,*
feathers like minor keys
      plinked on Sunday morning

fallen quietly into the birches' iron crèche,

awes to accompany midnight reels
of wordless repressions, a sense of badness in the solar
plexus, that tender wheel named elsewhere
as *soul-nest,* feeling there a flutter
of anguish, avian panic of cannot stay, cannot migrate.

I'm trapped, he'd said, before ascending the lighthouse, last day
of summer getaway, fried perch and drift glass,
      the gulls' intense need.

Did you feel it, he'd asked,
      the impulse?

Aliens, listeners and pollinators,
scavengers and singers, Dickinson's hope before returning
to her bolt of beyondness, the terror
of Civil War in her pen,

little sons, little daughters, little mothers, little fathers, Heaven-
on-Earth, forgive me
my quietude, ruinous in the sunshine
      of a quiet afternoon.

ANOTHER LANGUAGE

2018

A clutch of clicks assembles the *thirty minutes*
the little one lived, was nosed to the surface and carried
through grooves of currents, by fin and spume,
tensile spine arced to keep love aloft against the press of
orchestral sisters, oil-and-egg-colored,
scratched as heirloom mirrors. Vessels, reverse
her burden. Pause the wild clock.
Harpists, your song is the one
of bereft women in community centers knitting booties
for infant burials. Shoal of cardigans,
skein of empathy, final pearls are left unfinished
for a portal. Others surf and confess,
anonymous, in virtual rooms, *If I could have held mine like that,*
ministered to by stranger-witnesses,
logging off at daybreak as the acidic Salish Sea,
once potion, dissolves further the body.
Vocalizations in the bluish struggle. The waves' outrage
a balm, replaying the swum elegy. *Mother* or *Tahlequah* or *J35,*
her real name elsewhere, in another language.

THE LETDOWN

Pitter-patter of its little feet: morning
awakening against shutter. Someone in bed, signaling
C'mere. When the kiss opens, tips into
that mindless place. Wisteria druggy on a spear-tipped gate.
Stone pine grown accustomed to the city, protecting
the vast veranda. Shyness. Flood of
feel-good in the stream. Then the inability to feel the glint of it,
pitiable silver of *Was once.* The phantom
suckle. Sensation of being filled, of filling up, a perfume
the wisteria—April's ache—conducts.

HORIZON

The hatchlings wrestle from gum and yolk, sealed
envelope or leather-bound diary,
picking the lock with an egg tooth, which falls after a day,
and the horizon is compass, is the will to live
encoded for millennia, so they courage on with jellied
siblings toward the saline. Let there be not
confusion of photography or artificial white wave tips
of a Publix. The mother, in the birth-trance,
shed salty tears, scattered sand
for decoy nests, then disappeared forever.
When Jennifer, with her mellifluous accent, asked
if I had any kids myself, I said (too loud and braless) *I feel
as though I'm just becoming a person,* which was
too woo for the occasion. The one who survives out of two
thousand glimmerings will use Earth's magnets
to home to the same beach *(regression)* in maturity.

ARCADE

If I regard now a mule deer,
surprise in fescue,

if the deer in its individual dusk
looks back, scans the blue

and green wavelengths
of my bipedal blur,

comprehends it and stays.
If we're safe

in mutual presence, our ears
can lower and do.

If it's easy as resting by the fence
in wordlessness.

If the divine blue returns
assuredly in morning,

and contrails mingle
with day's snowy remnants

on the deepening tree line.
If root integrity holds

the mountaintop.
If safety and sleep mean the same

in some language lost
to a radioactive future.

If I was landed to guard the gap
that lets a deer slip through,

then my cortex is bathed
by good blue

as the deer skims grasses.
A goose *(soot-necked, rejected)*

is a periscope on steps,
and the fruit flies

of childhood, the depression
of them, wither too

before the laptop's emissions
in experiments.

THE BAT

How it careened, encircled by pokeweed
and burdock, a shyer voice
uncrushed, wings making Vantablack halos over
the smallest port sips,
sensuous in August tar, gooey
in humidity, like nights doing mascara
in the rearview in college, clubbing in leotards
to Depeche Mode, arguing
through a pay phone's filthy pinpricks.

Tonight, the neighbor's cat visits,
shifted from scythe-pupiled huntress to C-
shaped kitten, summer licking
her fur as the oak squiggles its vermin home,
moon projecting intimacy
as in the therapy room, that incident with the glass
veering into confession, erotic as Sexton's
crossed legs, her *Beyond it* expression.

The dead holly sat like omen
for months before some daisies came in
like a cavalier second wedding, the jolly bride
no longer fertile, niece fresh
from doing Ecstasy in the ladies', an awesome

dancer turning nineteen amid
extraordinary renditions, black sites,
face torqued as the DJ entrances her further
until she's blissed, brutal as a gargoyle.

ALBINO DEER

Stunning as noon sun or psychosis aftermath, vase
flung into the garden, but surely the milk glass
was speaking and the mother, she couldn't let it go on
terrorizing the household, could she?
White noise, attention span frail as a ghost crab
clattering into surf, washed backward into the mist
of Ansel's photographs, synth to soften a century,
gallows clouds fusing with Osipova's jetés in the Bolshoi.
From the green edge stepped nothingness, sobs
of snow from the orchestra warm-up (first post-
disaster performance) hushed by the soloing oboist,
slow whole notes, quarter notes hoof-black, O solemn
comet, you bride, you confusion, you phantom.

PATHWAY

I wiped my mouth clean and went, deranged,
into daylight, mincing (careful walk of the oft-falling)
to the Fontana dell'Acqua Paola
where a duck swam singly as if transformed into a crystal
of exquisite peace, in a cloudless basin.
Never mind the motorcycles' keen or idling exhaust,
the teenaged beauty's boyfriend taking, again
and again, her photograph against a red and ivory backdrop.
Feather or flesh, any veined thing
was absorbing the same sunbeam. I felt a neuron
pulse, a pathway changing course. Rain roads
and roads made by people, transient road the duck
made of her stylized blue, converging.
Our sensitivities, our natures, together just once. Healing,
the literature says, is relational. As the wound was.

BLUEBIRD

Of happiness: I knew it once in the blue
eye of a white horse a neighbor kept.

It answered to the lowliest signal,
walked a childhood's length toward me.

Not mine, though the childhood was
entirely. No mistake.

Eye a blue bell rung with animal kindness,
the fatal instinct children have

to go willingly toward
whatever hand opens.

In the blue air above me: that blue eye,
still as a jay mourned already.

Gray fretwork, a barn, air a bonfire
dwindling, my friend

in such vapor unrivaled by another,
though I didn't know what it meant *to compete.*

Pony going sway, almost
unseen, birch-white against birch trees.

POKEWEED

But first a mockingbird must strafe
the scene like an F-16, twirling seed into manure

shroud-gray and poured on an auspicious day
(Venus visible, sky whistle-clean)

shuffling overhead angelic favorites.
As the mourning dove sips its bitter bright, so too

the cardinal, whose pious silks resist the poison,
its shade recalling pickled beet picnics

of the 1960s. Civil War soldiers pressed its death
in handkerchiefs, used juice to ink letters

in a swoony script that's left the landscape, *hope*
and *sweetheart* leant in loops and flourishes.

Into Appalachian poverty salad go immature leaves,
twice-rinsed. Further vanished, the Algonquian

who roamed and river'd here, deviling feathers,
shafts of arrows garneted for courage.

Suspended in piss or spit, fat or yolk, dye
binds to bridle or dress, flamboyant as an hour-long

kiss beneath the Perseids' quicksilver tail flicks
or poke-painted horses galloping to war.

ECCE HOMO

In a field of unbelieving irises, the miracle's
not yet leaflet, reflex of thorns to shine like the buffed floors
of a hospital still new. Lens of placenta
once gazed through
gone, so too the milky buds like stalks on a snail.
Analog days presage the android. I boil
water and salt to douse the dandelions, tricking tooth to root,
a sinister impulse in an airy room.

Roses clutch their wire mother.
Vibrating, she and I once squared up in the kitchen,
so close we could've kissed, over money. Thereafter, echoes
of rage, double shifts of shame, flinch
of sun, muscles at ease only under a strip mall's
needles. Unlock a door,
and the Ponte Vecchio appears, smile of gold over the Arno,
splendor incarnate, balm for a body's briary silence.

THE GREEN

There is green, there is the green
of childhood, the green missing, the one,

the one green given to the priest's eyes
in the airplane aisle, Oh God,

there is green, the single
green pane smearing the backward

glare and breakneck present
of green going, green thrall of time

and lark landed, playing
greenly one tongue

undone to music, pendulum
of green *that was, that was,* I don't imagine

I'll return, surround of walnut hulls,
a tabled dollar, I've held on to

childishness longer than most, green loss,
the green, Oh God, it is the cause.

ACKNOWLEDGMENTS

Grateful acknowledgment is given to the editors of the publications in which these poems first appeared:

The American Scholar: "Cradle Language," "Fruitless," "Horizon," "Lackluster, 2002," "Marrow's in Vogue," "Pokeweed," "Red Lake," "Two Donkeys in Eternal Rain"
Australian Book Review: "Untitled, 1954"
The Baffler: "Study of Beet and Earring"
The Drift: "Explicit, 1976"
The Georgia Review: "Quiet"
Granta: "At Thirty"
Great River Review: "Escape to Fiji"
Image: "The Egg of Anything"
The Irish Times: "Black Swans"
The Kenyon Review: "The Bee, 2050," "Songbird," "Sumptuary"
Liberties: "Albino Deer," "Glass of Milk," "Ouroboros"
Los Angeles Review of Books, "The Green"
MIT Technology Review: "Search Field"
The New Republic: "The Bat"
The New Statesman: "Januaries"
The New York Review of Books, "Epic Rain"
New Welsh Review: "Bluebird"
The Oxford Review of Books: "Color Theory"
Poetry: "A Brief History of the Cocktail," "Eelish"
Poetry London: "The Lambs Are Not for Sale," "Lamentation Once Again"

The Poetry Review: "Among Barmaids," "The Skunk"
Port Magazine: "Afterglow"
The Progressive: "The End," "The News"
Raritan: "Black Cat"
Spirituality & Health: "Everything"
The Tablet: "Elk Moving, Midnight in the Great Sand Dunes"
The TLS: "Pathway," "Restoration"
Western Humanities Review: "I Love the Whole World"
The White Review: "Ecce Homo," "Pillow Talk," "A Violence"
Women's Review of Books: "Testimony"
The Yale Review: "The Letdown"

"Among Barmaids" received second prize in the 2013 National Poetry Competition from The Poetry Society (UK). "Bluebird" was included in a group of poems that received the 2013 George Bogin Memorial Award from The Poetry Society of America. "At Thirty" was made into a short film, supported by Motionpoems.

The epigraph to "Red Lake" is from Fernando Pessoa's *The Book of Disquiet,* translated by Richard Zenith (Penguin, 2001). "Red Lake" nods to Elizabeth Bishop's poem "One Art" (1976). The epigraph to "Quiet" is from the article "Three Billion North American Birds Have Vanished since 1970, Surveys Show." The phrase "a violence" is from Wallace Stevens's essay "The Noble Rider and the Sound of Words," delivered as a lecture at Princeton in 1941, published by Princeton University Press in 1942, and collected in *The Necessary Angel: Essays on Reality and Imagination* (Knopf, 1951).

I'm grateful for the Amy Lowell Poetry Travelling Scholarship, which gave me a year abroad, where some of these poems were written. Thanks also to Green Box for a residency where others were written. I thank Rowan Ricardo Phillips for selecting *A Violence* for the series. I thank my husband Patrick Mullen for his love, encouragement, and support.

PRINCETON SERIES OF CONTEMPORARY POETS

Almanac: Poems, Austin Smith

An Alternative to Speech, David Lehman

And, Debora Greger

An Apology for Loving the Old Hymns, Jordan Smith

Armenian Papers: Poems 1954–1984, Harry Mathews

At Lake Scugog: Poems, Troy Jollimore

Atom and Void: Poems, Aaron Fagan

Aurora Americana: Poems, Myronn Hardy

Before Our Eyes: New and Selected Poems, 1975–2017, Eleanor Wilner

Before Recollection, Ann Lauterbach

Blessing, Christopher J. Corkery

Boleros, Jay Wright

Carnations: Poems, Anthony Carelli

The Double Witness: Poems, 1970–1976, Ben Belitt

A Drink at the Mirage, Michael J. Rosen

Earthly Delights: Poems, Troy Jollimore

Erosion, Jorie Graham

The Eternal City: Poems, Kathleen Graber

The Expectations of Light, Pattiann Rogers

An Explanation of America, Robert Pinsky

First Nights: Poems, Niall Campbell

Flyover Country: Poems, Austin Smith

For Louis Pasteur, Edgar Bowers

A Glossary of Chickens: Poems, Gary J. Whitehead

Grace Period, Gary Miranda

Hosts and Guests: Poems, Nate Klug

Hybrids of Plants and of Ghosts, Jorie Graham

I entered without words: Poems, Jodie Gladding

In the Absence of Horses, Vicki Hearne

I Was Working: Poems, Ariel Yelen

The Late Wisconsin Spring, John Koethe

Listeners at the Breathing Place, Gary Miranda

Movable Islands: Poems, Debora Greger

The New World, Frederick Turner

The New World: Infinitesimal Epics, Anthony Carelli
Night Talk and Other Poems, Richard Pevear
The 1002nd Night, Debora Greger
Operation Memory, David Lehman
Pass It On, Rachel Hadas
Please make me pretty, I don't want to die: Poems, Tawanda Mulalu
Poems, Alvin Feinman
The Power to Change Geography, Diana O'Hehir
Prickly Moses: Poems, Simon West
Radioactive Starlings: Poems, Myronn Hardy
Rain in Plural: Poems, Fiona Sze-Lorrain
Reservations: Poems, James Richardson
Returning Your Call: Poems, Leonard Nathan
The River Twice: Poems, Kathleen Graber
River Writing: An Eno Journal, James Applewhite
The Ruined Elegance: Poems, Fiona Sze-Lorrain
Sadness and Happiness: Poems, Robert Pinsky
Scaffolding: Poems, Eléna Rivera
Selected Poems, Jay Wright
Shores and Headlands, Emily Grosholz
Signs and Wonders: Poems, Carl Dennis
Stem: Poems, Stella Wong
Stet: Poems, Dora Malech
Syllabus of Errors: Poems, Troy Jollimore
The Tradition, Albert F. Moritz
The Two Yvonnes: Poems, Jessica Greenbaum
The Unstill Ones: Poems, Miller Oberman
A Violence: Poems, Paula Bohince
Visiting Rites, Phyllis Janowitz
Walking Four Ways in the Wind, John Allman
Wall to Wall Speaks, David Mus
A Wandering Island, Karl Kirchwey
The Way Down, John Burt
Whinny Moor Crossing, Judith Moffett
A Woman Under the Surface: Poems and Prose Poems, Alicia Ostriker
Yellow Stars and Ice, Susan Stewart

GPSR Authorized Representative: Easy Access System Europe - Mustamäe tee 50, 10621 Tallinn, Estonia, gpsr.requests@easproject.com

www.ingramcontent.com/pod-product-compliance
Lightning Source LLC
Jackson TN
JSHW021527280825
90013JS00009B/7

POETRY

A RECKONING WITH PSYCHOLOGICAL AND ECOLOGICAL CRISES FROM A POET WHOSE WORK HAS BEEN PRAISED AS "BEAUTIFUL AND RIVETING" (*Los Angeles Review of Books*)

A poetic representation of PTSD and its evocative bewilderments, Paula Bohince's mesmerizing new collection, *A Violence*, is written at inflection points: a waking from dissociation borne from a harrowing childhood; a breakdown; and a struggle toward wholeness by means of mystified recollection amid ecological disturbances. Praised for poems that "reward enormously upon first encounter, and only more so upon subsequent reads" (*The Rumpus*), Bohince is here alert to surprise, the enthralling image "rushing through such wreckage a brain becomes." Contemplating vulnerability and resilience in the entwined human and natural worlds, with a voice precise and powerful, *A Violence* is a haunting collection that builds symphonically to recover a self "gone away," where the ordinary is imbued with transcendental significance.

"With a fiercely observant eye, and with disarming, wide-awake music, Paula Bohince considers what's to be made of all that's been diminished. Negotiating the achingly beauty and fragile persistence of a damaged world, *A Violence* is ecstatic, woeful, and gorgeous."
—Mark Doty, National Book Award–winning author of *Fire to Fire: New and Selected Poems*

"Paula Bohince's poems—urgent, melodious, and always surprising—articulate the known world in lines of stunning clarity. A book for every reader interested in the achievements of poetry today."
—Cynthia Zarin, author of *Next Day: New and Selected Poems*

Princeton Series of Contemporary Poets
Rowan Ricardo Phillips, Series Editor

Cover image: © Photo Josse / Bridgeman Images

Paula Bohince is the author of three previous poetry collections, *Swallows and Waves*, *The Children*, and *Incident at the Edge of Bayonet Woods*. Her poems have appeared in *The New Yorker*, *Granta*, *The New York Review of Books*, *The Times Literary Supplement*, and many other publications.

ISBN-13: 978-0-691-27776-9